DON'T WHISTLE
IN SCHOOL

DON'T WHISTLE IN SCHOOL

The History of America's Public Schools

Ruth Tenzer Feldman

LERNER PUBLICATIONS COMPANY • MINNEAPOLIS

In memory of Milton Tenzer and Sophie Posner Tenzer, and with heartfelt thanks to Michael Feldman and Margaret Goldstein

Author's interviews: Elizabeth Adams, Barbara Edwards, Stephanie Evans, Keith Feldman, Yvonne Hood, David Kirsh, Deidre Salcetti, and Christopher Logan Slough. Additional thanks to George Arnold, archivist at the Artemas Martin Collection of textbooks at the American University Library, Washington, D.C.

Lerner Publications Company
A division of Lerner Publishing Group
241 First Avenue North
Minneapolis, MN 55401 U.S.A.

Website address: www.lernerbooks.com

Library of Congress Cataloging-in-Publication Data

Feldman, Ruth Tenzer.
    Don't whistle in school : The history of America's public schools / by Ruth Tenzer Feldman.
        p.   cm. — (People's history)
    Includes bibliographical references and index.
    ISBN 0-8225-1745-0 (lib. bdg. : alk. paper)
    1. Education—United States—History. 2. Schools—United States—History. I. Title. II. Series.
LA212.F35 2001
370'.973—dc21   00-058789

Manufactured in the United States of America
1 2 3 4 5 6 – JR – 06 05 04 03 02 01

Contents

NEW WORLD ABCs

*All Blessings Come Down Even
From God.*
        —*The New England Primer,*
                                    1690s

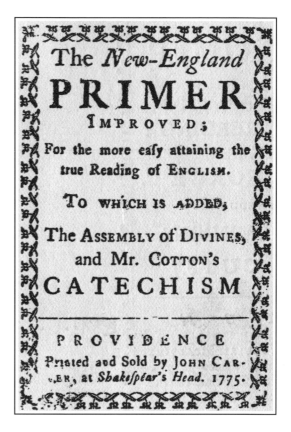

The *New-England*
PRIMER
IMPROVED;
For the more easy attaining the
true Reading of ENGLISH.

TO WHICH IS ADDED;

The ASSEMBLY of DIVINES,
and Mr. COTTON's
CATECHISM

PROVIDENCE
Printed and Sold by JOHN CAR-
TER, at *Shakespear's Head.* 1775.

In 1993 Christopher Logan Slough and three classmates at Fluvanna County High School in Palmyra, Virginia, decided to take Latin. Every school day for two years, the four students sat at a table in front of a television set. They watched a Latin teacher broadcasting live by satellite from her school in West Virginia. They asked her questions over the telephone and sent in their homework by fax. Christopher thought his Latin class was "really cool—one of my best experiences in high school." Taking Latin was "a fun concept."

"The Latin tongue is the Intent of my Mission" is how schoolmaster Thomas Morritt described the focus of his Charleston, South Carolina, school in 1728. Had Christopher Slough attended Morritt's school back then, Latin would have been his main, and practically his only, subject. There was no chance he would have learned about another of his favorite subjects in high school—photography. Indeed, Christopher's experiences in school are a far cry from those of boys his age in early America. Over the past four centuries, American schools have changed, along with changing ideas about what it means to be a well-educated American.

"FITTED FOR YE UNIVERSITY"

For wealthy American colonists first arriving from England in the early 1600s, Latin was the most important area of study. It was the scholarly language of Europe, used in theology, medicine, science, and foreign correspondence. In England as well as in North America, upper-class boys attended grammar schools, private schools for boys only that taught Latin and Greek. Boston Latin School, established in 1635, was the most famous grammar school in colonial America.

Boys usually started at Boston Latin at age seven or eight and stayed about seven years, learning enough Latin and Greek to pass the entrance examination for Harvard College (founded in 1636). Required reading included Ovid's *Metamorphoses* and Virgil's *Aeneid,* both in Latin. School was conducted year-round, and students attended whenever possible. The Latin master also employed an usher, an assistant teacher who taught English.

Not everyone in the early American colonies was supposed to learn Latin—just the upper classes—but almost everyone was expected to read the Bible. If schools in the colonies that became the original thirteen states had had an advertising slogan, it probably would have been this: Defeat the Devil—Learn to Read!

In 1647 in Massachusetts Bay Colony, the Puritans—the colony's dominant religious group—decreed the following:

> It being one cheife proiect of ye ould deluder, Satan, to
> keepe men from the knowledge of ye Scriptures . . . [every
> town with fifty households shall appoint someone] to teach
> all such children as shall resort to him to write & reade,
> [and every town of one hundred households shall] set up a
> grammer schoole to instruct the youth so farr as they shall
> be fitted for ye university.

Those who didn't attend grammar school usually learned to read
and write English at home. For a small fee, some children learned
English at "dame schools," also called "petty schools," run by women
from their homes. Beginning readers sometimes used a hornbook—a
paddle-shaped board that held a printed piece of paper beneath a sheet
of transparent animal horn. Most hornbooks were printed with the
alphabet and some religious writing, such as the Lord's Prayer. The
transparent horn protected the paper, which was expensive at that

The instructor in this dame school teaches domestic chores.

time. After about 1750, children learned the alphabet, numbers, and elementary reading skills from illustrated booklets called battledores.

COLONIAL CONDITIONS

Towns throughout New England and elsewhere in the colonies followed the example of Massachusetts's "ould deluder" law and established schools. Town officials tried to set up schools like those in Europe, but conditions in the New World caused them to make changes. With few students, fewer qualified teachers, and a shortage of money, the lines between grammar and dame schools blurred. Schoolmasters established "English grammar schools" and "general schools," which offered a mixture of Latin and English. Some dame schools offered elementary arithmetic and beginning Latin along with English. Some schoolmasters even allowed girls in Latin grammar schools.

The quality of education depended on how well each teacher was educated. In the early colonial days, the main qualification for a teacher was that he or she be religious. Schoolmasters (except women who taught at home) usually received bed and board, about $1 to $1.50 a week (half in provisions and half in money), and exemption from taxes and military service. Many colonial schools charged tuition, and each student brought wood for the fire during the winter term. Sometimes those who brought the least wood sat farthest from the fire.

Some towns paid for the education of their poorest children. Dedham, Massachusetts, set up a school that was free to all children there. Established in 1645, it was probably the first public school in America. It was built in the center of town and included a tower from which the students could watch out for Indian attacks. Dutch settlers placed a great value on education. In 1661 officials in the Dutch city of New Amsterdam (later New York) instructed schoolmaster Evert Pietersen that "the poor and needy, who ask to be taught for God's sake he shall teach for nothing."

Schools in some colonies were open all year. Others were divided into terms, with boys attending in winter, when there was less outdoor work to do, and girls attending in summer, when there was less housework to be done indoors. Schools operated by Quakers, a religious group based in Pennsylvania, ran from three to eleven months, usually six or seven. The Dutch school in Flatbush, New York, ran nine months straight, from September to June.

Some New England towns set up "moving schools" to reach as many children as possible. The town would be divided into quarters, and people in each section received a quarter of the school fund money, selected a place to hold school, and chose their own schoolmaster. The school then moved from one quarter of town to the next, spending one-fourth of the school year in each location. This practice led to the system still used by some high schools and colleges, in which the school year is divided into academic quarters.

The middle colonies, especially in the market towns of New Amsterdam and Philadelphia, Pennsylvania, had a variety of schools, in keeping with the various religious and cultural backgrounds of the colonists there. In Pennsylvania and New Jersey, the Quakers discussed education at their yearly religious meetings. They decided who would teach whom and what would be taught where. In Quaker communities, girls and boys were usually taught in separate schools. The Dutch West India Company (a firm authorized to colonize and trade in the New World) and the Dutch Reformed Church started New Amsterdam's first school in 1638.

Built around 1695, the Voorlezer's House (*voorlezer* is Dutch for "reader") on Staten Island in New York City is the oldest schoolhouse in the United States. Hendrick Kroesen, the first teacher there, instructed the children in his Dutch Reformed community in religious doctrine, reading, writing, arithmetic, and the history of the Netherlands. After British colonists gained power in New York, many children there studied English. A bilingual English-Dutch reader (reading textbook) was published in 1730.

In the South, many colonists lived in the countryside, on large plantations or isolated farms. Often they hired tutors or used servants to teach their children at home. Neighboring children sometimes gathered at an "old field school"—often a log shack built on land that was no longer good for farming and, therefore, was exempt from taxes.

Some teachers on plantations were indentured servants—people who had agreed to work for several years in exchange for the cost of their ocean voyage to the New World. Colonial newspapers sometimes ran notices that asked for the return of indentured teachers who had run away from their masters.

Thomas Jefferson's education was typical of the children of southern aristocrats. Jefferson attended a one-room schoolhouse with his relatives, but not with the plantation's slave children, who received no education. An exceptional student, Jefferson could read many of the books in his father's library by age five.

Jefferson had several tutors, from whom he learned the classics (Greek and Latin), social graces, and dancing. When he was fourteen, he went to James Maury's academy, one of several private schools in the colonial South. He spent two years there learning Greek, Latin, and other skills that would make him "a compleat gentleman." Afterward, he attended Virginia's College of William and Mary.

"THE BOY THAT IS GOOD DOES MIND HIS BOOK WELL"

The typical colonial school day followed a well-established routine. The citizens of Flatbush, New York, instructed their schoolmaster to ring a bell to start school, a practice that was probably widespread. The school day usually lasted for a few hours in the morning, then a few more hours after lunch. School rules in New Haven, Connecticut, required the schoolmaster to take the roll twice a day and to mark down absences and tardiness. New England boys were expected to bow when they entered and left school and to stay in their assigned seats. Everywhere in the colonies, school days usually began and ended with prayer.

When it was time for orthography—spelling—the whole class bellowed out each word in syllables, then the proper spelling. If a word were misspelled, the guilty classmate would be identified, or the whole class would have to spell the word again. When reading aloud, students were instructed to read fast, to mind the "stops and marks"—punctuation—and to speak up.

Schools made do with what was available. Often students wrote with sticks on a dirt floor. Some students wrote with soft stone on boards that had been blackened with a mixture of egg white and the carbon of charred potato. Other students used charcoal to write on thin pieces of wood. Since penmanship—good handwriting with fancy flourishes—was sometimes more important than correct spelling, students spent hours practicing writing. They copied passages into books of rag paper, using ink pens made from goose quills. Primers—reading books—explained how to make the ink, and students learned that brandy and salt would keep it from freezing or getting moldy.

Used in both church and school, primers were originally prayer books with an alphabet added. The most popular primer throughout the colonies was *The New England Primer,* which first appeared in about 1690. It included rhymed alphabets, religious essays and poems, and instructive questions and answers. Most homes had a copy of this primer; adults read it, too. Students had to buy their own primers, and they often wrote warnings like this one on the inside front page:

> Isaac Greenwood is my name,
> Steal not this book for fear of shame.
> And if this book should chance to roam,
> Just box its ears and send it home.

Latin grammar books were called accidences. The most popular one was written by Ezekiel Cheever, master of Boston Latin School from 1670 until his death in 1708. Cheever's *Accidence, a Short Introduction to the Latin Tongue* was the only schoolbook of completely American origin before the Revolutionary War.

Although all students learned to read and write, fewer students could cipher—do arithmetic. Arithmetic textbooks were rare. Instead, students learned rules and studied problems from "sum books," hand-printed by teachers. Most students did not progress beyond the "single rule of three," which is essentially basic algebra, as shown in this problem from a sum book: "If 13 yards of Cloth cost 39 dollars, how many yards of the same may be bought for 156 dollars?"

Teachers also used the Bible to teach reading, penmanship, spelling, and even arithmetic. They were expected to catechize their students—ask questions about religion for which answers were to be memorized—and were sometimes required to attend church services where students repeated the catechism.

For punishment, this boy must wear a dunce cap.

Most towns permitted schoolmasters to give "due correccions" in moderation, even for bad behavior out of school. Students who were simply unprepared for class were often punished as well. Boys might be hit with a birch rod, a whip, or a flat piece of wood called a ferule. Girls might have to stand in the corner or sit on a one-legged stool called a uniped. Children who misbehaved in dame schools were sometimes tapped on the head with a thimble; pinned to the dame's apron; or made to wear dunce caps, huge leather spectacles, or large labels that said "Idle Boy." Those in Dutch schools were rapped on the palm with a piece of wood. A common punishment for a boy was to have to sit with the girls.

ROLL CALL

Despite the "ould deluder" laws, many colonial children never went to a formal school, or attended for only a short time. Fewer girls than boys attended school, but many girls were self-taught. Mercy Otis Warren, for example, sat in on her brothers' lessons at home in Barnstable, Massachusetts, as their uncle tutored the boys for entrance into Harvard College. She also used the books in her uncle's library. Warren later became a noted historian and anti-British activist.

Apprentices—young people who were learning a trade from a skilled master—rarely attended school during the day, although some attended master-operated night schools. Benjamin Franklin learned one of his many professions, printing, as an apprentice, although he also had a few years of formal schooling. Many colonies required apprentices to learn to read and required that they be catechized weekly. Officials in the Massachusetts Bay Colony sometimes placed children in apprenticeships if their parents were not properly educating them.

Only a handful of African Americans appear to have attended school along with whites in New England. In Boston, Massachusetts, Cotton Mather, a prominent Puritan minister, set up a school for African Americans and Indians in 1717. Starting in the 1700s, Pennsylvania Quakers held monthly educational meetings for blacks, while in some Quaker schools black and white classmates studied together. Quaker abolitionist Anthony Benezet opened a school specifically for blacks in Philadelphia, while other Quakers supported schools for blacks in Virginia and North Carolina.

As for Native Americans, educators were primarily concerned with converting them to Christianity and urging them to give up native traditions. Religious organizations in England, such as the Anglican Society for Propagation of the Gospel in Foreign Parts, sent missionaries to convert the "heathens" of the New World, including Indians and African Americans. A few Indian schools were established, including the first Indian college (in connection with Hartford College) in 1654. At Elias Neau's school in New York City, open from 1705 to 1725, blacks, Indians, mulattoes—people of mixed race—and a few white apprentices attended together. Neau's students, who were mostly adult men and women, studied the Bible and learned to read.

LITERACY OF LIBERTY

In 1776 students at Boston Latin School published their own handwritten newspaper. Called the *Public School Intelligencer,* the newspaper included a sports section, puzzles, and school gossip. The cost of subscribing to the *Intelligencer* was one sheet of writing paper a week.

The boys of Boston Latin were still among the elite. Probably fewer than half of school-age American children got to attend school in the 1770s. Yet basic literacy was widespread in early America. Whether or not they had attended school, many colonists could read the Bible. That meant that they could also read newspaper accounts of Great Britain's treatment of the colonies, as well as pamphlets complaining about British rule.

Throughout the colonies, American teachers began to teach about independence. Some students organized independence demonstrations. In 1776 British soldiers hung the former schoolmaster of East Haddam, Connecticut, when they found their military plans encoded in Latin and Greek in his shoes. The schoolmaster's name was Nathan Hale.

LESSONS FOR
A NEW NATION

Preach, my dear sir, a crusade against ignorance; establish and improve the law for educating the common people.
—Thomas Jefferson, 1786

The Revolutionary War left many colonial schools deserted, damaged, or destroyed. In the years that followed, not only would these schools need to be rebuilt but they would also need to be redesigned to suit the new democracy—the newly created United States of America.

Congress realized that education was critical for the kind of citizens the new republic needed, stating that "religion, morality, and knowledge being necessary to good government and the happiness of mankind, schools and the means of education shall forever be encouraged" in the nation's new states and territories. Under the Ordinance of 1785, Congress divided frontier territories into townships, each with thirty-six lots measuring six hundred forty acres. Lot 16 (and sometimes two or three others) had to be sold for at least one dollar an acre, with money from the sale used to build and maintain schools. Some western territories, such as Montana, the Dakotas, and Washington, were required to establish free public schools before they could become states.

Some congressmen wanted to set aside land in the new territories for both schools and "the support of religion." Others argued against using government money for churches. The First Amendment to the Constitution, which became law in 1791, settled the debate. This amendment prohibited the establishment of a state religion, although debates long raged about this "separation of church and state" and whether religious education could be paid for with public funds.

SCHOOL THE AMERICAN WAY

The typical American school of the early nineteenth century was not much different from the typical colonial school. Students recited their lessons out loud, and teachers did not hesitate to administer punishment. At Daniel Drake's "blab school" in the Ohio River valley, "the fashion was for the whole school to learn & say their lessons aloud." Daniel's teacher used a wooden switch to prod, gently or otherwise, students who were silent. (Abraham Lincoln and his sister, Sarah, attended a blab school in Indiana.)

The fictitious schoolmaster Ichabod Crane, in Washington Irving's short story "The Legend of Sleepy Hollow" (1819–1820), "swayed a ferrule, that sceptre of despotic power." The real school Irving had attended in New York City had been taught by a Revolutionary War veteran who, like Crane, did not "spare the rod." (Since Irving hated to watch this punishment, which the teacher inflicted on boys after the girls were dismissed, he was allowed to leave when the girls did.)

Schoolwork, too, was much the same as it had been in colonial times, although early nineteenth-century students learned about the geography of the new United States. Using familiar tunes like "Yankee Doodle" and "Go Tell Aunt Rhody," children sang geographical facts about the nation. Songs usually included the name of a state, its capital, and the river that ran through the capital.

This illustration of fictitious teacher Ichabod Crane accompanied Washington Irving's short story "The Legend of Sleepy Hollow."

In the 1830s, William McGuffey created a set of reading books with different levels of difficulty. Although there were other readers, McGuffey's *Eclectic Readers* (1836, 1837) were among the most popular. Selections such as the story of George Washington and the cherry tree and descriptions of Washington as "the Moses of the United States" were designed to create an American identity. McGuffey was a Presbyterian minister, and his books, like most textbooks then, had a Protestant bias. They included moral lessons, such as "Respect for Sabbath Rewarded," and instructed poor students to be satisfied with their station in life.

Students studied orthography, often consulting Noah Webster's dictionary and his spelling guide nicknamed the *Blue-Backed Speller.* First published in the late 1700s, this speller was used well into the twentieth century. Spell-downs (spelling contests) were common, with students vying for prizes—usually maps or pictures. Some students learned to spell words by memorizing a sentence, such as "**A r**at **in**

Noah Webster wrote a spelling book for students and later several dictionaries.

the **h**ouse **m**ay **e**at **t**he **i**ce **c**ream." Sometimes, entire communities had contests to see if a local celebrity could "spell down" the teacher. Modern spelling bees harken back to this activity.

Established in 1821, Boston's English Classical School was the first place we would call a high school. Offering instruction to older children, the school was supported by taxes and controlled by public authorities. By the 1850s, high schools were operating in about eighty American cities. The schools usually offered a classical program, emphasizing Greek and Latin in preparation for college; an English program that included literature, writing, and about sixteen other subjects (such as astronomy, history, and logic); and a two-year "normal" program to train students to become teachers. Because parents often needed teenage children to help support the family with paying jobs or to work on the family farm, few students attended high schools. Fewer graduated.

REVOLUTIONARY SCHOOLS

Some early nineteenth-century schools were more innovative. In New York City, a group called the Free School Society adapted a highly detailed system devised by Joseph Lancaster, an English Quaker.

In Lancaster's system, a school of several hundred children could be managed by just one teacher. More advanced classmates—called monitors—taught those who knew less.

Adapting Lancaster's model, the Free School Society built a number of schools (which later became the basis for New York's public school system), numbered them, and made them all alike. Classrooms for the youngest students were on the first floor, girls' classrooms were on the second floor, and boys' classrooms were on the third. Each classroom had long desks that seated ten to twenty students, and each displayed Joseph Lancaster's motto: "A place for everything and everything in its place."

The school day (9 A.M. to 2:30 P.M.) started with a religious reading, recitation of school rules, and inspection of students for cleanliness. A boy with a dirty face might be washed by a girl in front of his classmates. Every half hour was carefully planned, with lots of dictation—writing down spoken words—and memorization.

Students were told exactly what to do, how to do it, and when. One manual showed monitors how to hand books to classmates and how students should read and turn the pages so that the books lasted longer. Both monitors and teachers started dictation by stating: "Attention, take slates, clean slates, hands fixed, take pencils." Students repeated each spoken word or phrase in unison before writing it. Beginning writers, called the "sand class," wrote their letters with sticks in sand on their desktops. Their desks had holes at the ends, through which excess sand could fall into drawers.

Classmates who excelled received certificates and honorary labels. Those who misbehaved received humiliating punishments, including suspension from school, which at that time meant hanging from the school roof in a basket or sack.

Corporal (physical) punishment was forbidden at the New Harmony boarding schools in New Harmony, Indiana, but life there wasn't easy. Dressed in simple uniforms, students there led very regimented lives and rarely saw their parents. Sarah Cox Thrall

New Harmony, Indiana

complained about the medicine students were forced to swallow. She remembered: "At regular intervals, we used to be marched to the community apothecary shop, where a dose that tasted like sulphur was impartially dealt out to each pupil." Thrall described the school's healthful but unappetizing food and remarked: "I thought if I ever got out, I would kill myself eating sugar and cake."

New Harmony was an experimental community, created in 1825 by reformers who believed in equality for women, in a classless society that would eliminate poverty, and in equal educational opportunities for all children. New Harmony's schools attracted children from as far away as Philadelphia and New York.

The schools were based on a system established by Swiss educator Johann Pestalozzi. He believed that children learned best not by drill and punishment but by observing the world around them and by positive motivation. In his schools in Switzerland, Pestalozzi proved that all children could learn, regardless of social background, economic class, or gender. Poor girls could become just as well educated as rich boys, he showed.

New Harmony's "infant school" taught two- to five-year-olds in a style similar to later kindergartens. The school for students ages five to twelve offered girls the same education as boys. Children over twelve attended an adult school, usually held at night. Students learned many academic subjects at the schools and mastered at least one occupation. Although the colony at New Harmony eventually broke up, many of its teaching methods influenced later educators.

SCHOOLS FOR THE MASSES

By the 1830s and 1840s, European immigrants were moving into American cities. Many American farmers were also moving from rural areas to cities, enticed by factory jobs and discouraged by the

The children in this class play a game called "windmill." Two circles of children—one inside the other—would move in opposite directions. Then the children in both circles would change directions when instructed to do so.

Young women working at Lowell, Massachusetts, textile mills could attend evening classes at their boardinghouses.

depletion of farmland in eastern states. Lowell, Massachusetts, was one famous factory town that enticed workers—mostly teenage girls—to its textile mills. Concerned town officials tried to educate the girls, making sure that public schooling was available to them. And because many of these young workers were Irish Catholic immigrants, Lowell (and other cities) experimented by incorporating Catholic schools into its town school system.

A prominent supporter of such schools for "the masses" was Horace Mann, a lawmaker and member of the Massachusetts State Board of Education. He believed that education would help working people improve their lives and would make them better citizens. "It may be an easy thing to make a republic," he wrote in 1848, "but it's a very laborious thing to make republicans." His "common school" movement pushed for state-supported, mandatory education (public schools) for all children, at least at the elementary level.

Protestant churches also supported the common school movement. Church leaders saw school as a way to bring religion and morality to common people, and they provided thousands of Bibles to public schools. Not everyone was comfortable with the Protestant influence on schools, however. Bridget Donahue, a devout Catholic, refused to read the King James—Protestant—version of the Bible in her public school in Maine, believing that to do so was a sin. The school board expelled her; a state court decided that the school board was right. According to the court, Bridget's school had used the Bible to educate her in general and not for religious purposes (which would have violated the First Amendment).

CONGRESS LAND

In new western states and territories, settlers established school funds, as dictated by the Ordinance of 1785 (although in many cases the funds were squandered by townspeople who pocketed the money or used it to make other improvements to the town). School fund trustees—usually local taxpayers—decided where, when, and how children went to school.

Although some teachers were men, many communities hired a "schoolmarm," often a single, young woman sent from the East to bring Christian education to frontier children. Dispatched by religious organizations, these women often taught both public school and Sunday school. If money from public funds ran out—which it frequently did—teachers either closed their schools or set up their own "subscription schools," paid for by the parents of the students.

Frontier schoolhouses were makeshift institutions, sometimes with horse shelters, outhouses, and a stove or fireplace, but little or no furniture. Most frontier children went to school only a few months each year, generally in summer and winter, since spring and fall were taken up with farmwork. Rarely did the school term begin and end with the same number of students. Classmates dropped out or moved on when their families left town.

At the typical frontier school, children brought lunch in a tin pail, usually an emptied container of syrup or molasses. The youngest children sat close to the teacher, usually sharing a two-person desk (when desks were available) with another child of similar age and the same sex. Often, girls sat on one side of the room and boys on the other. Sometimes boys and girls had separate recess times.

Students helped each other, and class work involved a lot of memorization and dictation. Reading, arithmetic, penmanship, and grammar took up most of the day's instruction. Students wrote on slates—thin pieces of gray rock—with a pencil made of soft stone. It was customary for boys to spit on their slates and rub them clean with their sleeves. Girls wiped their slates with rags, which they wet in a water bucket.

The frontier school was not all memorization and dictation, though. One Indiana school had a "post office box," in which classmates dropped "written questions on any subject which interests their minds." Their teacher, Cynthia Bishop, remembered the first question: "What do men get drunk for?"

In some frontier schools, older boys challenged male teachers. As the school trustee for an Indiana town told the hero of Edward Eggleston's novel *The Hoosier School-Master* (1871): "Want to be a school-master, do you? . . . Why, the boys have driv off the last two, and licked the one afore them like blazes. . . . They'd pitch you out of doors, sonny, neck and heels, afore Christmas."

In a practice called "barring the door," older boys barricaded themselves in the schoolhouse before school started. If the teacher couldn't get into school, classes were cancelled that day. Eggleston's fictitious schoolmaster took back his barricaded school one day by dropping sulfurous powder down the chimney.

Frontier children who misbehaved would certainly be punished, although not always with unhappy results. In *The Adventures of Tom*

Sawyer (1876), Mark Twain described a school similar to one he attended in Hannibal, Missouri, in the 1840s. Twain's hero, Tom, entered school once while the teacher, Mr. Dobbins, "was dozing, lulled by the drowsy hum of study." Dobbins woke up, whipped Tom with a switch for being late and for talking to Huck Finn, and made him sit with the girls. Since Tom wanted to be near a girl named Becky, he was delighted.

Mark Twain's fictional Tom Sawyer, left, disliked school and sometimes skipped class. This illustration depicts a scene for which Tom is famous, where he entices a friend to help him paint a fence.

"PUT OFF BY THEMSELVES"

Relations between Native Americans and whites ranged from friendly to ferocious in the nineteenth century, as white settlers pushed westward, sometimes slaughtering Indians and driving them from their homes. Starting with the Removal Act of 1830, the U.S. government officially pushed eastern tribes onto western lands, where they were supposed to be "civilized" according to Anglo American standards. Although President Andrew Jackson claimed that this plan of "removing the aboriginal people" contained arrangements for schools, federal aid was meager.

In 1817 Cherokee leaders went to Washington, D.C., to ask for schools for their children. Working with Protestant missionaries, the U.S. government agreed to establish a boarding school—Brainerd Mission—in Chickamauga, Georgia. The curriculum was based on white, Christian ideals. Teachers gave Cherokee students English names and taught them in English. In the evenings, the students learned religious doctrine. The school day was exhausting, lasting from 5:30 A.M. to 9:00 P.M. When students were not studying, they did farm chores. Brainerd Mission became a model for other Indian schools throughout much of the 1800s.

One Indian boarding school, established by the Methodist Episcopal Society in Fort Leavenworth, Kansas, focused on manual labor. Five days a week, Indian boys and girls spent six hours a day in class and six hours pursuing "practical arts" such as farming and cleaning. Relying mostly on missionary support, more than one hundred Native American schools were operating by the mid-1800s.

Like Native Americans, African American children attended school in some places, but rarely with white classmates. Philadelphia used public funds to support separate schools for black students. Some cities operated private schools for African Americans, including the African Free School in New York, run by the Manumission Society, a group devoted to the abolition of slavery. In 1824 James McCune Smith, an eleven-year-old student there, recited for the Marquis de

Lafayette, a Revolutionary War hero. By all accounts, the marquis was impressed.

An occasional private school offered education to children of all colors. In 1833 Prudence Crandall accepted Sarah Harris, a mixed-race student, into her academy for girls in Canterbury, Connecticut. After parents threatened to withdraw other students from school, Crandall closed the academy and opened a school exclusively for African American girls. Neighbors threw manure chips at the students and attacked the school. Fearing for her students, Crandall closed that school, too.

African Americans in frontier schools had varying experiences. For example, two black children attending public school in Watsonville, California, in the early 1850s were "put off by themselves . . . no matter how much they out-spelled" their classmates. When Henry and Alfred Magee attended school in Macoupin County, Illinois, white parents complained to the school board. The boys then switched to a school for African American children and were later welcomed in

Prudence Crandall hoped to offer education to African American girls.

their Racine, Wisconsin, high school as the only blacks among the three hundred students there.

Education for African Americans in the South was haphazard and hazardous. Most southern blacks were slaves, with no rights at all. Some slave owners thought education led to rebellion; others thought slaves should be literate enough to read the Bible or to help with clerical work. In the 1830s, several southern states passed laws forbidding the education of slaves, fining whites for selling books to slaves, and prohibiting free blacks from attending school. At least one white woman spent a month in jail "for assembling with negroes to instruct them to read and write." Despite these laws, some black children did learn to read and write. A black teacher named Julian Troumontaine held secret classes for free blacks for fifteen years.

Katie O'Connor, who was white, gave lessons to her playmate Susie King Taylor, a slave, with Susie's promise that Katie's father wouldn't find out. Susie then used her education to write passes that allowed her grandmother, also a slave, to travel off the plantation. Robert Glenn remembered that his owner's son secretly "furnished me books and slipped all the papers he could get to me and I was the best educated Negro in the community without any one except the slaves knowing what was going on."

In his book *Up from Slavery* (1901), educator Booker T. Washington recalled:

> I had no schooling whatever while I was a slave, though I remember on several occasions I went as far as the schoolhouse door with one of my young mistresses to carry her books. The picture of several dozen boys and girls in a schoolroom engaged in study made a deep impression upon me, and I had the feeling that to get into a schoolhouse and study in this way would be about the same as getting into paradise.

STRIVING TO
MAKE THE GRADE

Rodney . . . was reduced . . . to a needy boy . . . poorer [than his friend who] had a chance to learn a trade . . . while he was utterly without resources, except in having an unusually good education.
—Horatio Alger Jr., *Cast upon the Breakers,* 1893

By 1860 the United States seemed more like two countries than one. The North had a booming industrial economy, supported in part by newly arrived European immigrants. The South relied on farming, supported by three million black slaves. As the nation grew larger, many Northerners wanted to abolish slavery in the western territories. Southerners opposed restrictions on slavery and threatened to withdraw from the United States if slavery were prohibited. One public school in New York exchanged letters and scientific specimens with another school in Virginia, as a way to demonstrate "the indivisibility . . . of the Union." Despite such efforts, war broke out between the North and the South in 1861.

The war disrupted schooling on both sides, as teachers and students quit school to become soldiers. At Central High School in Philadelphia all senior students graduated, even those who had left to serve with the Union army. Nearly all the schools in the South were closed as Union troops swept through the countryside. Despite a shortage of paper and other school supplies during the war, a few Southern schoolbooks were printed. One included this arithmetic problem: "If one Confederate soldier can whip 7 Yankees, how many soldiers can whip 49 Yankees?"

When Union troops seized the Sea Islands off the South Carolina coast, plantation owners there fled, leaving their slaves behind. The U.S. Treasury Department (which took over the plantations) and relief groups from the North established the Port Royal schools there for about ten thousand slaves. One teacher from the North, a free black woman named Charlotte Forten, wrote that she "never before saw children so eager to learn."

In March 1865, one month before the war ended, Congress created the Freedmen's Bureau, designed to give emergency aid to newly freed Southern blacks. Immediately after the war, the bureau, along with charitable groups from the North, helped more than ninety thousand black children enroll in public schools.

Shortly after the war ended, a black soldier from Ohio came to Booker T. Washington's town in West Virginia. No free school for African Americans had yet been established there. So the newly freed slave families paid the veteran to teach them, and he moved from family to family. "I looked forward with an anxious appetite to the 'teacher's day' at our little cabin," recalled Washington.

Union troops remained in the South as part of Reconstruction, Congress's plan to rebuild the region economically, enforce new civil rights laws, and bring the Confederate states back into the Union. In 1866 men of the Fifty-sixth Colored Regiment, stationed at Helena, Arkansas, bought thirty acres of land near their camp and deeded it to a group of Indiana Quakers. The Quakers built the Southland Institute, a school for lost and abandoned black children.

Many white Southerners opposed efforts to educate blacks. They burned African American schools and beat teachers and students. Edmonia Highgate, who taught in Lafayette Parish, Louisiana, in 1866 wrote: "There has been much opposition to the School. . . . My night school scholars have been shot but none killed."

Still, by 1877, when the Reconstruction period ended and Union troops left the South, more than half a million black children—about one-third of school-age blacks—were enrolled in school. Black colleges were founded around this time, including Tuskegee (founded by Booker T. Washington), Howard, and Fisk.

HOMESTEAD SCHOOLS

Farther west, Americans by the wagonful had been settling the frontier for several decades. The Homestead Act of 1862 had given them a reason to move to the frontier and stay there. Anyone over age twenty-one who was the head of a family and a citizen (or intended to become one) could get one hundred sixty acres of public land for

The chemistry laboratory at Tuskegee Institute in Alabama, founded in 1881

$1.25 an acre, provided he or she lived on the land for five years and farmed it. From 1862 to 1900, the act provided land to about five hundred thousand families.

The Calof children were part of a tiny community of Russian Jewish homesteaders in Overland Township, North Dakota. Their mother recalled:

> Our first schoolhouse was a simple one-room building. . . . It served four families. In the winter the teacher slept in the schoolhouse, and often the children . . . would find her still asleep. Under these circumstances the school day began with a recess while the teacher dressed and cooked her breakfast.

Formal education varied on the frontier, depending on the teacher's education, textbooks available, and community preferences. For some parents, a basic understanding of reading and spelling was sufficient "book learning" for their children. Others sent their children to school as soon as a teacher could be found and as often as the youngsters could be spared from activities required for the family's survival.

Laura Ingalls Wilder's experiences, which she described in her *Little House* books, were typical of many frontier children. Starting at age seven, Laura attended one-room schoolhouses in Minnesota and Dakota Territory. In 1882 she passed a test given by the school superintendent and earned a certificate to teach school nearby. She was only fifteen.

As a student, Laura carried lunch to school in a tin pail, brought her own slate and schoolbooks, and sat two to a desk with another girl, separated from the boys. For the school exhibition at the end of the term, she did "mental arithmetic." Dividing 347,264 by 16 in her head, Laura came up with 21,704. (Was she right?)

Frontier classmates struggled with greater hazards than math problems, though. When Angeline Brown became a schoolmarm in Tonto, Arizona, she wrote in her diary: "Quite a school . . . 23 pupils in a house 10 × 12, dirt floor, brush sides . . . & no door! And only seats for 12." One day Brown's school had a visitor. "I was hearing a Geography class . . . looked down . . . & there lying on my dress skirt in a ray of sunlight was as hideous a reptile as I've ever seen." The Gila monster literally became the teacher's pet. "I stroke his scaly back with a pencil & he likes it apparently," Brown wrote.

Weather was another hazard at frontier schools. A blizzard that hit the northern plains in January 1888 is sometimes called the "school-children's storm," because many were caught at school. More than two hundred people died, most of them children. Minnie Freeman's heroic actions when her schoolhouse collapsed in the storm inspired a song called "Nebraska's Fearless Maid," or "Thirteen Were Saved."

During the blizzard, fuel ran out in a schoolhouse in Jerauld County, Dakota Territory. Fred Weeks tried to guide his classmates and schoolmarm to a house about four hundred twenty feet from school. Blinded by the storm, they missed the house by six feet and buried themselves in a haystack. The class sang, told stories, and kept each other awake until a search party found them twelve hours later. Some children lost their feet to frostbite, but everyone survived.

FEW CHANGES IN THE ROLL

As schools for white children grew more numerous, even in remote areas of the United States, opportunities for nonwhites remained limited. In the Southwest, children of Mexican heritage often were prohibited from attending school with whites. It didn't matter whether these children were recent immigrants from Mexico or members of families that had lived on the land for generations, long before the region became U.S. territory.

Schools for native Alaskans discouraged tribal traditions. After the United States purchased Alaska from Russia in 1867, missionaries went to Alaska, determined to educate "heathens with hellish practices." Children at one boarding school in Sitka were allowed to speak only English and had to sign contracts saying that they wouldn't see their families for five years.

Native American boys at the Carlisle School wore military-style uniforms.

At government-sponsored Indian boarding schools, often established in abandoned military forts, military officers served as teachers, and Native American children were forced to attend. Government workers called Indian agents sometimes withheld rations or money owed to Indian families on reservations if they refused to send their children to school.

At the Carlisle Indian Industrial School in Carlisle, Pennsylvania, Indian traditions were forbidden. "Seven years I was there," recalled a student from Taos, New Mexico. "I set little letters together in the printing shop. . . . They told us Indian ways were bad. They said we must get civilized." One eleven-year-old Hopi boy remembered his first year—1899—at an Indian boarding school this way:

> I had learned many English words and could recite part of the Ten Commandments. I knew how to sleep on a bed, pray to Jesus, comb my hair, eat with a knife and fork, and use a toilet. I had learned that the world is round instead of flat, that it is indecent to go naked in the presence of girls, and to eat the testes of sheep or goats. I had also learned that a person thinks with his head instead of his heart.

New England missionaries to Hawaii devised a written version of the Hawaiian language, then printed textbooks and a Bible in Hawaiian—mostly in an effort to convert the native peoples to

A government-run elementary school in Hawaii

Christianity. Queen Liliuokalani, Hawaii's last monarch, attended a missionary-run boarding school, sometimes called the Royal School, where she was given an English name, Lydia.

With U.S. annexation of Hawaii in 1898, a system of government-sponsored schools was established there. However, some sugarcane plantation owners questioned whether the children of workers should even go to high school. As one planter complained:

> Why blindly continue a ruinous system that keeps a boy and girl in school at the taxpayers' expense long after they have mastered more than sufficient learning for all ordinary purposes?

SOMETHING OLD, SOMETHING NEW

In some schools in the late 1800s, students continued to learn in the same way their parents had. They were taught to memorize and recite and rarely to think for themselves. Thinking, however, was precisely what "progressive" educators wanted students to do. They believed that students learned best when they were interested in the material they studied. Teachers in progressive schools were supposed to act as guides, showing students how to solve problems by experimentation and analysis.

New educational movements were nothing new in the United States. In 1873 St. Louis had opened the first public kindergartens, based on those established by Friedrich Froebel in Germany. Froebel's educational philosophy involved nurturing young children's spirits. He introduced twenty educational toys—he called them "gifts"—including sewing kits, paper weaving kits, and origami folding papers. The gifts were designed to teach children about the relationships between art, mathematics, and nature. (The Milton Bradley Company manufactured Froebel's gifts under the name Bradley's Kindergarten Material.)

Francis Parker, a school superintendent in Quincy, Massachusetts, introduced her Quincy System of education in the late 1800s. In her program, students took field trips to study geography and figured out arithmetic not by studying rules but by moving objects like chestnuts and toothpicks. Teachers supplemented textbooks with magazines, newspapers, and other materials. In one class, students "exercis[ed] their powers of observation and thoughts" about flowers. They recited poems about flowers, talked about how to nurture plants, used flowers to learn about numbers and patterns, painted pictures of flowers, and wrote stories about them.

In 1896 John and Evelyn Dewey established the Laboratory School in Chicago to test their theories of progressive education. The Deweys believed that a child's education at school should develop from life experiences. In the Deweys' elementary school, the youngest students learned stories and games based on familiar activities. Older

John Dewey was a leader in the progressive education movement.

students played grocery store and sold fruit and sugar, from which the rest of the class made jelly. Students in each age group expanded their knowledge around a central theme. For example, the ten-year-olds focused on colonial history.

In the early 1900s, U.S. Steel built a mammoth plant in Indiana and created the town of Gary to house its workers. The new public school system there was a concrete example of progressive education. Students in Gary schools were not assigned to permanent desks. They each had individual educational programs and worked at their own pace. In one class, girls ages nine to twelve focused on a motorcycle. They studied how the motorcycle operated, learned about the physics of riding a motorcycle, and used words related to motorcycles in their spelling lessons. Gary students even helped maintain and operate their school buildings. If they wished, they could attend Saturday tutoring classes in most subjects. The Gary schools were open to everyone in the community, all day, year-round.

"MORAL AND SOCIAL LESSONS"

Often it was the students themselves who introduced new activities into schools. For instance, in the mid-nineteenth century, American high school students began to organize sororities, fraternities, secret societies, and sports teams, many modeled after similar organizations at colleges and private British boarding schools. The first interscholastic baseball team was organized in 1859 at Worcester High School in Massachusetts. High school football was first played on an organized basis in the 1880s. Early school sports teams were highly competitive, and games were often very rough.

Other extracurricular programs included school newspapers, glee clubs, literary societies, and debate teams. Reading clubs developed into school libraries. In rural schools, corn- and cotton-growing contests were popular, as were garden clubs and children's fairs. Originally for farm children, 4-H clubs organized in rural schools beginning in the 1890s.

Civic leaders and faculty members gained control of high school sports programs in the early 1900s. The adults saw sports as a way to "build character" and to make high school more attractive to students, their parents, and the community. In 1903 Luther Gulick Jr., the director of physical training for New York City's public schools, organized the Public School Athletic League. Citing the "physical benefits and moral and social lessons afforded by properly constructed games and sports," the league introduced athletic classes, team sports, and athletic badges for boys into the city's public schools.

Girls did receive some physical education, but only because educators believed that exercise would strengthen girls for childbirth and motherhood. Otherwise, few girls were allowed to participate in sports, even into the mid-twentieth century.

"I LOVE SWEET AMERICA"

Immigrants escaping desperate poverty in Europe were amazed to find free public schools in the United States—schools that would give their children a chance to make it in the new nation. For Mary Antin, whose family came from Russia, "going to school was the fulfilment of my father's best promises to us."

New York City's Public School (PS) 188 gave immigrant students a crash course in English. Among the publications that the new English-speakers might read was *Student and Schoolmate,* a monthly magazine. It published Horatio Alger's serialized stories about people struggling to survive in urban, industrial America. The heroes of most Alger stories were poor working boys from New York City who struck it rich because of their diligence, honesty, and luck—and because they could read and write.

Particularly in big cities like New York, immigrants still lived in poverty, without proper facilities for sanitation. Each week, teachers in New York City gave hundreds of baths to students from overcrowded tenements, hoping to discourage the spread of lice. Some schools taught children how to brush their teeth, and school nurses

Young and old immigrants from Eastern Europe learn English. Most newcomers were eager to learn American ways.

treated children with contagious infections such as ringworm—conditions that might go untreated at home.

With each new wave of immigrants, city schools became more crowded with students from many different backgrounds. Civics became a required course, designed to teach an increasingly diverse population about the American political system. In 1892 students learned the newly written Pledge of Allegiance to the American flag. Chicago first established student government in its high schools in 1895, partly as a way to maintain order among different ethnic, social, and economic groups.

STILL MISSING

But while the United States strove to "make the grade" as an industrial nation, little was done to bring children of every background

This illustration from the 1890s shows children in a New York City school saluting the American flag. Civics was an important part of the educational program.

and ability into the same schoolroom. Disabled children were frequently sent to special schools, including the American Asylum for the Education of the Deaf and Dumb in Connecticut, the Perkins School for the Blind in Massachusetts, the New York Institution for the Deaf and Dumb, and the Massachusetts School for Idiotic and Feeble Minded Youth. Cleveland started the first classes for "backward children" in its public schools in 1878. Chicago established the first public school class for children with physical disabilities around 1900. The "special class" movement gradually caught on in other public schools as well.

Schools continued to bar nonwhite children, including those of

Asian descent. In 1905 San Francisco's school board decided that the mixing of "children of Japanese or Mongolian descent . . . with Caucasian children is baneful and demoralizing in the extreme." San Francisco sent the Asian children to "Oriental schools," while other cities sent them to "colored schools" with African Americans. Martha Lum, an American-born girl of Chinese descent, was denied entrance to the school for white children in Rosedale, Mississippi. She took her case to the Supreme Court and lost.

Whether they were separated from whites or not, nonwhite children were often assigned to vocational programs. Teachers often dismissed their abilities to learn anything beyond basic manual skills. One educator in California suggested:

> As the Mexicans show considerable aptitude for handwork of any kind, courses should be developed that will aid them in becoming skilled workers with their hands. . . . Teach every boy how to make inexpensive furniture for the home. Boys should be taught to make use of discarded tin cans in

The Indiana Institute for the Blind, Indianapolis, Indiana

the development of useful kitchen utensils. Girls should be trained to become neat and efficient house servants.

In the *Forward,* a newspaper for Jewish immigrants, a writer described a similar situation in New York's public schools. He wrote: "The main subject is *Discipline;* obviously school authorities believe that poor children are incapable of becoming anything but clerks, so they must be taught to obey, not to think."

Black students were the ones most likely to attend segregated (separate) schools, a system upheld by law. An 1896 Supreme Court decision in the case of *Plessy v. Ferguson* allowed separate schools for whites and blacks as long as the facilities were equal. But schools for blacks were usually much poorer and offered far less education than was available for white students. Because of poverty and discrimination, many southern black children didn't go to school at all. Nate Shaw, a poor farmer, summed up the effects of segregation this way: "When I was deprived of book learnin, right there they had me dead by the throat."

FACE FORWARD

By the early twentieth century, most schools operated on the now-familiar American model. They were divided by grade and stayed in session nine months of the year. Classrooms usually had forty to forty-eight desks, bolted to the floor and facing the teacher's desk and blackboard. Most teachers were women who had at least had some formal education in teaching. Report cards and homework became standard classroom features. New inexpensive printing techniques and paper made it possible to mass-produce textbooks, and school districts provided them for free.

Students practiced penmanship to prepare for good clerical jobs. They had elocution lessons—complete with a system of dramatic gestures—to learn to be effective public speakers. Other lessons focused not on career training but on moral character. "Scientific temperance instruction," for instance, warned students about the dangers of drinking. In one popular demonstration, teachers put calves' brains in a glass jar, then poured in a bottle of alcohol. As the brains turned from pink to a sickly gray, teachers warned that this would happen to the brains of students who drank "Satan's brew."

World War I (1914–1918) brought other changes to the classroom. Intelligence tests like the Stanford-Binet, developed to evaluate army recruits, were later used to test schoolchildren. Although several school systems already offered low-cost or free lunches to their students before the war, school lunch programs spread rapidly when army physicals revealed an alarming rate of malnutrition in eastern cities. The main carbohydrate in these early school lunches was white bread (also an excellent material for spitballs).

By 1918 every U.S. state had compulsory education laws. More students were in school than ever before. In all, about three-quarters of school-age American children attended school for an average of ninety days a year.

THE HEAD OF THE CLASS

Teachers and parents expected us to learn but not to think for ourselves; we expected to be taught.

　　　　　　　—Beverly Cleary

In Beverly Cleary's autobiography, *A Girl from Yamhill,* she recalls that one day after Labor Day she walked with her mother to the two-story redbrick Fernwood Grammar School:

> Mother left me with other first-graders in the basement, where teachers lined us up, two by two. . . . Someone blew a whistle and called out, "Mark time!" Imitating other children, I pumped my knees up and down. "March!" Led by the first-grade teacher and still pumping our knees, we marched up the stairs to our classroom, where we were each assigned one of forty desks in five rows of eight, each row bolted to two boards so individual desks could not be moved.

While some schools of the 1920s adopted progressive methods (the Los Angeles public schools even held a geography class in an airship), many schools, like the one children's writer Beverly Cleary attended in Portland, Oregon, remained more traditional. She and the other first graders wrote in cursive. When Beverly held the pencil in her left hand, the teacher put it in her right one, telling Beverly she must not write with the left. Beverly practiced folding paper as an exercise in following instructions and learned to add and subtract using blue cardboard counters the size of nickels. She learned to read from two books her parents were required to buy—*The Beacon Primer* and *The Beacon First Reader*—each costing fifty-two cents.

Punishments hadn't changed much over the years. When Beverly let her mind wander, the teacher "swooped down and whipped my hands with her frequently used weapon, a metal tipped bamboo pointer." The teacher also had misbehaving children sit on a stool facing the corner, stay in the coatroom, and "crouch in the dark cave" under the teacher's desk.

OUT WITH THE OLD

But in many other ways the classroom had changed. When Beverly was in second grade, a person from the Portland telephone company came to teach the students how to use newly invented dial telephones. Five years later, when Beverly's mother complained that her daughter's handwriting was hard to read, Beverly's seventh-grade teacher seemed unconcerned. She "replied that before long most people would use typewriters."

John Tigert, a U.S. commissioner of education, also spoke of technology in the classroom. "Within the celluloid film lies the most powerful weapon for the attack on ignorance the world has ever known," he stated. Speaking in 1922, Tigert was referring to educational film strips, by then in use in dozens of school districts around the country. New machines, from automobiles to movie cameras, had entered American life—and the American classroom.

By the 1920s, the United States was a fast-paced industrial society. Advertisements for new products and labor-saving devices were everywhere. Commercialism even entered the schoolhouse, although students didn't always know it. For instance, school bands and orchestras became commonplace in American schools in the 1920s, but not just to provide cultural enrichment. By encouraging schools to form bands, manufacturers could sell more band instruments.

The National Bureau for the Advancement of Music, working closely with an association of piano manufacturers, promoted piano playing and instrumental music in school. The bureau wrote booklets on how to develop school bands, provided music and materials, and promoted national contests. The first national contest for high school bands was held in Chicago in 1923, as part of the Music Industries Chamber of Commerce convention. In 1926 the Bureau for the Advancement of Music sponsored its first national contest. The winning

School orchestras and bands became popular in the 1920s.

John Scopes, left, *and his father, Thomas*

high school band received a bronze-and-mahogany trophy, thirty inches high and valued at one thousand dollars.

New scientific ideas entered the classroom, but not without controversy. One revolutionary new idea was the theory of evolution, put forth by British naturalist Charles Darwin. Darwin's studies showed that plants and animals adapt and change over time in order to survive, and that the human species developed over millions of years from simpler animals and organisms. That theory contradicted a belief contained in the Bible—and frequently taught in American classrooms—that God had created life on earth in six days.

Darwin's theory offended and outraged many religious Americans. In 1925 Tennessee passed a law that prohibited the teaching of evolution in its public schools. In Dayton, Tennessee, high school biology teacher and football coach John Scopes challenged the law by reading this passage from a biology book to his class: "We have now learned that animal forms may be arranged so as to begin with the simple one-celled forms and culminate with a group which includes man himself."

Scopes was arrested. About one hundred reporters covered his trial, which was broadcast over another new and hugely popular invention, radio. William Jennings Bryan, a former presidential candidate, was Tennessee's attorney. Clarence Darrow, a nationally famous lawyer, defended Scopes. Not one scientist was allowed to testify at the trial, and Scopes was convicted and fined one hundred dollars. The tug-of-war over religion in the classroom, and what should be taught to America's children, continued.

STRUGGLING TO STAY IN SCHOOL

Beverly Cleary remembered how "in October 1929 the stock market crashed. Except for school, everything seemed to come to a halt." As factories shut down and banks failed, people lost their jobs, their homes, and their life savings. In the 1930s, the country fell into the Great Depression.

With their parents unemployed and homeless, more than two hundred thousand children roamed the country as drifters. Others barely managed to stay in school. In 1931 teachers in Chicago's schools fed eleven thousand hungry students a day. The school superintendent there pleaded with the governor of Illinois: "For God's sake, help us feed these children during the Summer."

Many schools shortened the school year, let teachers go or didn't pay them, or simply closed. In 1933 Congress set up the Federal Emergency Relief Administration, assigning teachers to country schools that would otherwise have to close down. Another federal relief program, the National Youth Administration, gave part-time, night, and summer jobs to more than one million students, so that the students could help support their families without dropping out of high school.

Weather made the Great Depression worse for those who lived in

During the Great Depression of the 1930s, the nation suffered a high rate of unemployment. These children in St. Paul, Minnesota, picketed on behalf of their out-of-work parents.

the Dust Bowl—part of the Great Plains that was struck by drought from 1931 to 1935. Then, from 1936 to 1940, howling winds carried away topsoil and made farming impossible. With barely enough money to travel, about three hundred sevety-five thousand destitute midwesterners managed to reach rich farm areas in Southern California. But there they found that jobs were scarce, pay was meager, and living conditions for migrant workers were horrible.

The U.S. government built emergency camps in California, where the "Okies"—refugees from Oklahoma and other Dust Bowl states—lived in one-room tin cabins and tents on wooden platforms. The children at Arvin Federal Camp, known as Weedpatch Camp, enjoyed hot showers, flush toilets, and breakfasts that cost a penny a day.

Going to the local public school was a different story, however. Many of the camp's children could not read or write. Most teachers ignored the poor children in their baggy overalls and dresses made of chicken-feed sacks. Other teachers forced them to sit on the floor, while wealthier local children sat at the desks. Myrtle Dansby wrote this poem about her school:

> The teachers nag
> And look at you
> Like a dirty dish rag.

Everywhere, it seemed, the children heard shouts of "Okie, go home!"

Leo Hart, the school superintendent, decided to take the Weedpatch children out of public school and to educate them without cost to the local taxpayers. In September 1940, Hart, fifty Weedpatch children, and eight teachers built the Arvin Federal Emergency School from surplus bricks and scrap lumber. They turned orange crates into desks, chairs, and shelves. They did their own plumbing, plastering, carpentry, and electrical wiring. In October the children planted crops and began to raise livestock. By the time the school's cafeteria was

Transplanted Oklahoma children at Weedpatch Camp near Bakersfield, California

completed in the spring of 1941, the children were drinking milk from their own cows and eating their own vegetables, eggs, and beef.

About two hundred students attended the camp school that first year. Half the children went to classes in the morning, while the other half finished building the school and tended crops. After lunch, the two groups traded places.

The school's principal, Peter Bancroft, even bought a surplus C-46 military airplane and taught the students aircraft mechanics. Any student who maintained a grade of 90 percent or better in arithmetic was allowed to drive the plane along a makeshift runway. Students who studied hard got to "dig in the hole," which was later turned into a swimming pool.

César Chávez—a Mexican American who later started America's first successful farmworkers' union—was not so lucky during the depression. After his parents lost their farm in Arizona, the family moved to California, where they picked carrots, cotton, and grapes wherever they found work. Chávez once counted sixty-five elementary schools he had attended, sometimes for only a week or a day.

MAKING DO AND DOING WELL

Other children, like Kenneth Hassebrock, lived through the depression with relative ease. Kenneth attended Ledyard Consolidated School in rural Iowa. His school was a new three-story brick building with a gym, several large classrooms for grades one through twelve, and indoor plumbing. Kenneth got used textbooks on credit and returned them at the end of the year for a few cents' charge. His favorite activity was shooting marbles on the school playground. Like many students in rural areas, Kenneth rode the school bus. He remembers:

> The buses we used were . . . homemade vehicles that displayed the genius of self-expression. . . . [T]he only requirements were that each bus had to have four wheels, be self-propelled, and students had to be able to get inside and survive a ride of several miles over unimproved county roads.

An early school bus

In 1939 school administrators and truck manufacturers agreed on the basic construction for school buses. They chose National School Bus Chrome as the yellow paint to be used only for school buses.

School also continued uninterrupted for Beverly Cleary. When she graduated from the eighth grade, the principal "handed each of us a small buff card, our first adult library card, a symbol marking the end of childhood." At Ulysses S. Grant High School, Beverly busied herself with social clubs and studies, including the requirement each year to memorize one hundred lines of poetry.

SCHOOL ON THE HOME FRONT

Yoshiko Uchida had nearly finished college in her native California when Japan bombed Pearl Harbor, Hawaii, in 1941. The U.S. government declared war on Japan, formally entering World War II (1939–1945). The government soon passed the Civilian Exclusion Order, forcing Japanese Americans—considered a threat to the United States—into internment camps. Yoshiko and her family were sent to Tanforan Assembly Center, where she lived in a horse stall for five months and taught second grade. Her students were eager to learn. She recalls:

> They were longing for a normal routine and needed school to give them the sense of security and order that had been snatched away from them so abruptly.

Before George Takei (*Star Trek*'s Mr. Sulu) and his family were sent to an internment camp, they were housed temporarily at Santa Anita Racetrack near Los Angeles. George started kindergarten there under the grandstand:

> We were housed in the stables there for about four months. . . . Ironically, all my real memories of Santa Anita

During World War II, the school at the Tule Lake Relocation Center in Newell, California, provided classes for children of Japanese descent.

were fun memories. . . . I was too young [to understand that] I lived where the horses lived.

One-quarter of the people in internment camps were school-age children. Most of them were teenagers, who graduated from camp high schools, usually barracks made of thin wooden frames and tar paper. Classmates brought chairs from their apartments or used benches made from scrap lumber. Every school day, students at the Manzanar camp, about ninety miles east of Fresno, California, saluted the flag and sang "My country, 'tis of thee, sweet land of liberty," although they were far from free.

Throughout the rest of the country, about three hundred thousand teachers left their jobs to join the military or to work in factories or offices supporting the war effort. With fewer teachers, many classrooms were overcrowded, and some schools closed.

David Kirsh, who attended elementary schools in Philadelphia, Cincinnati, and Detroit during the war, remembered how the war seemed to inspire unity and patriotism in the classroom. One of his classmates was a boy from war-torn England who had been sent to safety in the United States.

Like millions of other schoolchildren, David and his classmates bought twenty-five-cent stamps to paste into books. When filled, the books could be traded for defense savings bonds. Hannah Mason, who went to school in a small town in New Jersey, "used to go door to door to sell defense bonds and stamps. . . . I would get the bonds from school usually. We had contests—which class would sell the most."

The war brought air-raid drills to school and rationing—limits on purchases of food, gasoline, and other materials. Even bubble gum was scarce, because most of it was sent to the troops. When a candy store in Detroit somehow acquired bubble gum, David and his classmates rushed there. They were each allowed to buy two pieces.

In Willie Morris's fourth-grade class in rural Mississippi, each student had to pray twice a day for the U.S. troops. He rememberd:

We would all begin by blessing our soldiers and then rip-
ping into the Germans and the [Japanese]. Once Spit [a
classmate] began his prayer by saying, "Dear Lord, thank
you for the bombs that ain't fallin' on us."

LIFE WITH DICK AND JANE

After World War II, the United States entered a period of prosperity
and experienced a booming birth rate. During the 1950s, California
opened a new school on the average of one a week, but it still didn't
have enough classrooms. Classmates crowded into schools in new
suburbs. Eighty percent of first graders learning to read met two fictional friends, Dick and Jane.

Dick and Jane (with no last name) were featured in a series of
books created by Zerna Sharp and William Gray. With upbeat stories,
simple sentences, and bright illustrations, the books were based on
progressive educational theories that children learned best when encouraged to be imaginative.

Millions of young schoolchildren read about six-year-old Dick, his
sisters Jane (five) and Sally (three), their parents, and their pets: Spot
the dog, Puff the cat, and Tim, Sally's teddy bear. Dick and Jane
lived in a middle-class suburb, and nearly all their adventures ended
happily. Every few years, the books' illustrators updated the family's
car and drew Jane's dresses based on those in current mail-order cata-
logs. Dick and Jane received thousands of letters through the publishing company, and "they" wrote back. Children could also buy
Dick and Jane valentines, Christmas tree ornaments, party napkins,
and other book tie-ins.

Like the Dick and Jane books, *My Weekly Reader* (which had started
in the 1920s) became popular in the 1950s. Created by Eleanor Johnson, the director of elementary schools in York, Pennsylvania, this children's magazine featured different reading levels for different grades.

None of these publications could compete in popularity with television, however. As soon as *Howdy Doody,* the first major television

show for children, aired on December 27, 1947, children seemed to be glued to the set. During the 1950s, children's shows such as *Captain Kangaroo, Ding Dong School,* and *Watch Mr. Wizard* attracted young viewers. By 1959 forty-five educational television stations were operating in the United States, including some run by public school districts.

EXTRAORDINARY CLASSROOMS

A few lucky students, particularly in New York, attended out-of-the-ordinary schools in the 1950s. One specialized school included classes in sailing skills, taught on the *Schoolship John W. Brown,* docked at Pier 73 in New York City. From 1952 to 1956, Elizabeth Adams went to New York City's High School for the Performing Arts (the basis for the 1980 movie *Fame* and later television shows). She says her experience there was "incredibly wonderful."

The special public schools in New York required students to pass an entrance examination. For admission to the High School for the Performing Arts, students had to show talent in music, dance, or drama—the school's three departments. Twice every year, each student presented a performance project before at least one teacher, to show progress and to stay in the school.

Elizabeth won a slot in the music department. She commuted nearly an hour by subway to get to the school, a five-story building that "always looked like it was falling apart," she remembers. About four hundred students, from all over the city and from all backgrounds, attended. Their day was divided into four academic classes and four performance classes. The work was hard, and many students went on to become professional performers. Elizabeth ran for class president against future movie actor Richard Benjamin—and lost.

THE NEW THREE Rs

Although suburban teenagers in the 1950s usually enjoyed well-run, well-funded schools, complete with academic and social clubs, children in poorer neighborhoods faced a different life with their classmates. Some students joined gangs that vandalized schools and assaulted teachers and other students.

In response, parents and teachers sounded the alarm about declines in educational standards. The "three Rs" in New York City's public schools, wrote the *New York Daily News* in 1953, were no longer "reading, 'riting, and 'rithmetic," but instead were "rowdyism, riot, and revolt."

The 1955 movie *Blackboard Jungle,* based on a book of the same title, featured "juvenile delinquents" who grew up in the nation's poorest urban neighborhoods. In the movie, students in Chicago's fictional North Manual High School are ethnically diverse and poor. One teacher refers to the school as a "garbage can." Another teacher, a white World War II veteran, is beaten by his students before a black student, played by Sidney Poitier, comes to his rescue.

DUCK AND COVER

In the post-war era, the Soviet Union began to force its communist political system on other nations in Eastern Europe. Determined to stop the spread of communism, the United States entered the Cold War, a period of nonviolent conflict with its former World War II ally. The era was marked by distrust and hostility directed at communism and the Soviet Union.

Fear of communist influence swept through American society, even into the classroom. The 1950 booklet "How Red Is the Little Red Schoolhouse?" argued that progressive educational methods were introducing communism into schools. Teachers were required to take loyalty oaths, and their teaching methods were watched carefully. One member of the Indiana State Textbook Commission even tried to get the book *Robin Hood* removed from classrooms. The reason? The book's hero robbed from the rich and gave to the poor—an idea that resembled efforts to redistribute wealth under communist systems.

Cold War activities included preparations for nuclear attack. Civil defense leaders showed students how to survive such a disaster, and

Duck-and-cover drills were common in the 1950s. Schools directed these drills as preparation for nuclear attack from the Soviet Union.

students drew maps of their cities to show probable zones of damage and radiation fallout patterns. Air-raid drills were regular events. During the drills, students filed into their school's fallout shelter or ducked under tables and desks, covered their heads, and tucked into protective huddles, supposedly to shield themselves from a nuclear blast.

RACING THE RUSSIANS

On October 4, 1957, the Soviets launched the first man-made satellite—*Sputnik I*—into space. A month later they launched

Sputnik II, which carried a dog. Americans were astonished. How could the Russians have gotten into space first? What had happened to the United States's supposed superiority in science and technology?

A year later, *Life* magazine published articles about two sixteen-year-olds: Stephen Lapekas of Chicago and Alexei Kutzkov of Moscow. The articles explained that Alexei's school (Moscow School 49) demanded a lot from him and that good grades were the most important thing in Alexei's life. Stephen's American school (Austin High School) seemed to demand little from him. He didn't take school very seriously, was failing geometry, and spent his spare time practicing with the school's swim team. Although the same age, Alexei was two years ahead of Stephen academically.

Alarmed American parents demanded that public schools put more emphasis on science and mathematics, so that the United States could compete with the Soviet Union. Education was a matter of national defense, many believed.

"New math" was introduced shortly afterward. In this short-lived program, students did not memorize formulas and rules of calculation but instead learned mathematics by discovering "such properties of relations as reflexiveness . . . and transitivity." In his song "New Math," songwriter Tom Lehrer joked sarcastically that new math was so simple that "*only* a child can do it!"

OPENING THE SCHOOLHOUSE DOOR

In these days, it is doubtful that any child may reasonably be expected to succeed in life if... denied the opportunity of an education.
    —*Brown v. Board of Education,* 1954

THE LITTLE ROCK NINE

Textbooks in the 1950s emphasized the nation's fight for freedom abroad during World War II. They also portrayed a "melting pot" society, in which Americans of every culture and background enjoyed the blessings of prosperity and democracy. However, in some places in the United States, minorities were still barred by law or custom from sitting in the same classrooms with whites. Many people decided that the time had come to end segregation in public schools.

THE QUESTION OF EQUALITY

A major stumbling block to opening schoolhouse doors remained the *Plessy v. Ferguson* decision of the nineteenth century, which allowed "separate but equal" schools for whites and blacks. In the early 1950s, the National Association for the Advancement of Colored People

(NAACP) brought several lawsuits, arguing that the *Plessy* decision violated the Constitution's Fourteenth Amendment, which guarantees that all people will be treated equally.

In 1954 the Supreme Court decided five of these segregation cases at once. They all became known by the shortened name of *Brown v. Board of Education.* The nine justices unanimously concluded that separate schools for whites and blacks were, by their very nature, unequal. The opportunity for every child to get a good education was at the heart of American democracy.

LITTLE ROCK'S ANSWER

Some whites-only schools opened their doors willingly after the court decision. Others did not. The most violent confrontation occurred on the first day of school in September 1957 at Central High School in Little Rock, Arkansas. In response to the Supreme Court ruling, Little Rock's school board had selected nine black students to attend all-white Central High.

Arkansas governor Orval E. Faubus opposed integration and had sent the National Guard to prevent the black students from entering the school. One of the students, Elizabeth Eckford, accidentally arrived before the others. The guardsmen watched as angry whites spat at Elizabeth and threatened to kill her. Elizabeth ran back to a bus stop, where two white people helped her get on a bus for home. When the other eight students arrived, they were also forced to leave.

To enforce the law, President Dwight Eisenhower reluctantly sent one thousand soldiers to escort the nine students to school and keep them safe. According to Melba Pattillo, another of the black students:

> On my third trip to Central High, I rode with the 101st in an army station wagon guarded by jeeps with turret guns mounted on their hoods and helicopters roaring overhead. With the protection of our 101st bodyguards, we black students walked through the front door and completed a full day of classes.

In 1957 National Guard troops lined the streets to prevent black students from entering Central High School during the nation's first desegregation attempt in Little Rock, Arkansas.

The other black students were Terrence Roberts, Jefferson Thomas, Thelma Mothershed, Minnijean Brown, Carlotta Walls, Gloria Ray, and Ernest Green. They each had a bodyguard. When another student threw acid in Melba's eyes, her bodyguard, Danny, flushed them out with cold water and saved her sight. She continues:

> When one of us had a major problem, they brought in a three-hundred pound 101st guard nicknamed Goggles. With nightsticks and other equipment strapped at his side, he made the kind of shield that fended off even the most hard-core segregationists. We grew to love him because being with Goggles meant a safe day no matter where you went.

Harassment continued throughout that first year. In one classroom,

Melba found broken glass and peanut butter spread on her assigned seat. In December, Minnijean Brown was tripped in the cafeteria, and her bowl of hot chili landed on two of her harassers. Minnijean was the one suspended. Until then, crowds inside and outside the school had chanted: "Two, four, six, eight, we ain't gonna integrate." After Minnijean left, they added: "One down and eight to go." Despite this harassment, senior Ernest Green became Central High School's first black graduate the following May.

To prevent further integration, Governor Faubus closed Central High School for a year. When the school reopened in September 1959, Sybil Jordan Hampton, newly arrived from Springfield, Missouri, was one of five black students selected to attend. She remembers:

> And so I began my tenth-grade year as the only black student in a class of over six hundred at Little Rock Central High School. . . . I don't remember anyone standing outside the school heckling. . . . I wasn't afraid of being attacked in the halls. . . . What we lived in 1959 was total isolation. People didn't talk to you. . . . The only [white] student that I ever had any friendly relations with was from France.

Sybil thought she got a good education at Central, and by the time she graduated "black students were getting to know the white students."

"THE PROBLEM WE ALL LIVE WITH"

As the 1960s began, the promise of a melting pot society, in which everyone enjoyed democratic freedoms, was still slow in coming. When New Orleans was ordered by a court to integrate its schools, six-year-old Ruby Bridges was selected to become the only black student at William Frantz Public School, five blocks from her house. On her first day there in 1960, Ruby and her mother were driven to school by four federal marshals. Police kept back angry onlookers. Ruby remembers:

> As we walked through the crowd . . . I was surrounded by
> the marshals. People yelled and threw things. . . . When we
> climbed the high steps to the front door, there were police-
> men in uniforms at the top. The policemen at the door
> and the crowd behind us made me think this was an
> important place. It must be college, I thought to myself.

Novelist John Steinbeck saw Ruby walking through the crowd and
wrote about it in his book *Travels with Charley* (1962). Inspired by
Steinbeck's account, artist Norman Rockwell made a painting called
The Problem We All Live With. Published in the January 14, 1964,
issue of *Look* magazine, the painting shows Ruby escorted by marshals. The wall next to them is stained by splattered tomatoes,
thrown by an angry mob.

Most white parents reacted to Ruby's arrival by taking their children out of the school, leaving Ruby as the only child in her first-
grade classroom. The few white families who kept their children in
school were pelted with rocks and eggs. Yolanda Gabrielle, one of the
young white students, was frightened by "those ladies who yell so
ugly."

After a few months, the protests calmed down. In the spring,
Ruby's teacher managed to have a few white first graders meet with
Ruby for part of the day. By second grade, Ruby's class had both
black and white students.

Asian Americans fared better in the classroom but still encountered
prejudice. Abby Soong, born in California to Chinese parents,
described her school in the 1960s this way:

> I was probably one of three Asians in my class in my gram-
> mar school, and I remember being made fun of a lot. It
> was very painful. . . . When everyone played cowboys and
> Indians, I would always be made the Indian because of my
> black hair. . . . So they would braid my hair and shoot me,
> and I said "I don't want to die. . . ." [They said,] "You have
> to cause you have black hair."

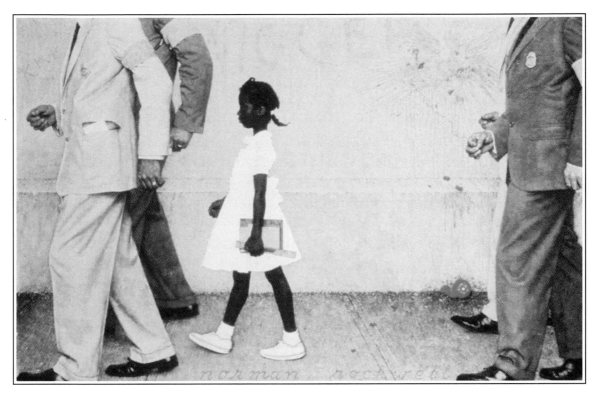

Norman Rockwell's painting **The Problem We All Live With**

Around the same time Ruby and Abby were going to elementary school, Emmi Whitehorse, a Navajo girl, went to a Bureau of Indian Affairs boarding school near her home in New Mexico. She remembered:

> I hated it. We were marched around like cadets. . . . It was very lonely. In the dining room, we were required to sit boy-girl, boy-girl, and that was torture. . . . Some of the teachers were very demeaning and made us feel ashamed of our culture. We were forced to wear uncomfortable dresses and hose. . . . We couldn't wear our hair loose. At Christmas . . . one year we all got Barbie dolls. . . . We all thought we were supposed to look like her.

DICK AND MIKE?

In 1965—one hundred years after the Civil War ended—Dick and Jane made friends with their new African American neighbors: Mike, his twin sisters, Pam and Penny, and their parents. Mike was just like Dick, and the twins were much like Sally.

While some American communities were like Dick and Mike's fictional town, many were not. Neighborhood schools stayed segregated because the neighborhoods themselves were segregated. How could communities comply with Supreme Court decisions such as *Brown v. Board of Education* when blacks and whites lived in different places?

One way to bring black and white students together was to bus them to schools outside their neighborhoods. During the 1960s and 1970s, many school districts tried the busing approach, either voluntarily or because they were ordered to do so by a court of law.

Court-ordered busing of black students to previously all-white high schools in Boston, Massachusetts, touched off violence in and out of school. As a result, students at Boston's Charlestown High School had to walk through metal detectors, installed to find weapons, on the first day of busing there. Lisa McGoff, a white student returning to Charlestown, decided to attend school regardless of the police officers lining the sidewalks, helicopters hovering in the air, and snipers on the rooftops. "I don't care if they bring the whole Army in here," she said. But when she saw the metal detectors, she felt that Charlestown wasn't her school anymore. She called it an "alien place . . . ruled by judges, bureaucrats, police."

Cassandra Twymon, a black student bused to Charlestown, dressed well for her first day because she knew she would likely be on television. But Cassandra's spirits sank as she stood in line at the metal detectors. Cassandra and other black students later wrote to the judge who had ordered the busing. They asked to meet with him about problems with the busing program, explaining:

We are writing this letter on behalf of the minority students of Charlestown and South Boston High Schools. . . . There are . . . blacks and whites that are afraid to attend these schools for the simple reason that they will get picked on in that they are black or white. . . . Education is the most important thing to us because we can't live without it.

The judge politely declined their request for a meeting.

"THE TIMES THEY ARE A-CHANGIN'"

In the 1960s and 1970s, American students realized that they could have a voice in political matters. Many African American students joined the antisegregation fight, including half a million students who boycotted New York City's public schools to protest segregation there in 1964. In 1968 about three thousand Los Angeles students held a

Older students assist younger students studying in a Berkeley, California, classroom. In November 1971, the Berkeley school district was one of the first to voluntarily desegregate through busing.

"blowout" to protest poor conditions in schools with mainly black or Mexican American enrollment. The protesters walked out of classes, threw rocks, set fires, and clashed with police.

Many student protests involved demonstrations against the Vietnam War. To show their opposition to the war and to resist military service, many young men burned their draft cards (government-issued cards that identified them as available for military service).

Even junior high students joined the movement against the war. In 1965 Mary Beth Tinker, John Tinker, and Christopher Eckhardt wore black armbands to class at Warren Harding Junior High in Des Moines, Iowa, to mourn those who had died in Vietnam and to support a truce. School officials had warned them that students who wore armbands would be suspended, and they were. The three students then challenged the armband rule in the Supreme Court, and they won the case. The court ruled that "students are entitled to

Students rally for peace in the Vietnam War era.

freedom of expression of their views" and that classrooms should be a "marketplace of ideas," so long as students did not intrude on the rights of others or the work of the school.

Some student protests ended tragically. At an antiwar protest at Kent State University on May 4, 1970, in the midst of tear gas, hurled stones, and angry shouts, National Guardsmen fired shots at student demonstrators. Thirteen protesters were shot. Four were killed. For American students, in the words of a popular protest song of the 1960s, the times were certainly a-changin'.

THE GLOBAL CLASSROOM

<http://www.ed.gov>

As the nation celebrated two hundred years of independence in 1976, some schools continued to teach in basically the same ways they had in the 1950s and 1960s. Elementary school students stayed with one main teacher in a single classroom for most of the day. In middle school or junior high, students had a different teacher for each subject.

But some districts experimented with alternative schools and alternative programs. "Open schools" became popular, especially in North Dakota and in major urban areas like Washington, D.C. These schools didn't have walls between classrooms. Teams of students, sometimes in different grades, worked together at "learning centers" to focus on subjects like math, art, creative writing, science, and social studies. Instead of letter grades on report cards, teachers issued checklists showing each student's skills.

"Magnet schools" first began as a way to desegregate public schools. By specializing in one area of study, the schools attracted students from outside the neighborhood. For example, Prince Georges County, Maryland, developed magnet schools devoted to French, communications, technology, the classics, and other special areas.

Later some districts created same-sex academies, such as San Francisco's Marina Middle School. Educators who ran the schools believed that separating boys and girls reduced social pressures and distractions in the classrooms and improved academic performance. One school, See Forever in Washington, D.C., even operated a restaurant. Students there learned academic skills as well as cooking skills. They attended school ten hours a day but got to keep some of the restaurant's profits.

Students no longer focused entirely on the traditions of white English Protestants in school. Instead they learned about the many ethnic and religious traditions that make up the U.S. heritage. In essence, they learned about others and about themselves. Schoolchildren in the tiny town of Scammon Bay, Alaska, for instance, learned to read and write Yup'ik, their native language. Public schools in Hawaii taught the Hawaiian language, while the Rough Rock Demonstration School in Arizona taught some classes in Navajo. The Rough Rock curriculum also included "cultural identification" activities, such as visits from tribal medicine men and classes in traditional Navajo weaving, leatherwork, and basketry.

Ah-Bead-Soot, a ten-year-old Native American student at the Chief Leschi School on the Puyallup Reservation in Washington State, described her classroom this way:

> My teacher is white, and I think she's learning more about Indians than we're learning about whites. We're learning

some of our old language, and our history. If you don't learn history, you'll make the same mistakes.

NEW TOOLS

High school students used computers in the classroom as early as the 1960s. The first computers were very large and were usually located at big companies and universities. Students accessed the computers through the phone lines, using a machine called a Teletype.

One of the first computer programs in the classroom was computer-assisted instruction (CAI). With this system, the computer would flash a question on the terminal screen, and the student would type an answer on a keyboard. If the answer were right, the computer would flash another question. If the answer were wrong, the computer would help the student find the correct answer. This teaching method was similar in some ways to the repetitive drills used in classrooms two hundred years earlier, but CAI allowed students to learn at their own pace.

In the late 1960s, students at Muzzy Junior High School in Lexington, Massachusetts, learned to use a new tool, a computer language called LOGO. Developed at the Massachusetts Institute of Technology by Seymour Papert, the program was designed specifically to help children learn. The Muzzy students used it to translate English into Pig Latin. They also used it to direct robotic "turtles" to draw designs on paper and on computer screens. The LEGO toy company later used LOGO in some of its robotic toys.

Most American students didn't know about computers in the 1960s, but they all knew about television. A longtime fixture in American homes, televisions were about to play a greater role in education. In 1967 Congress created the Corporation for Public Broadcasting to help fund educational television programs. The effort quickly paid off in the form of *Sesame Street,* which first aired on November 10, 1969. Designed like a fast-paced television commercial, the award-winning show taught numbers, letters, and basic

Matt Robinson and Loretta Long talk with Jim Henson's Muppets on Sesame Street, *a television series for preschoolers.*

vocabulary words to preschoolers, with the help of well-loved puppet characters. More innovative shows followed, including *The Electric Company* in 1971 (which taught reading) and *3-2-1 Contact* (science) and *Square One TV* (math) in the 1980s.

Television even entered the classroom itself. Students watched news broadcasts as part of their studies, as well as instructional programs sent by satellite. Students in some schools even produced their own television programs and broadcast them to their classmates.

On January 28, 1986, thousands of students watched television in school as Sharon Christa McAuliffe and six astronauts shot skyward in the space shuttle *Challenger.* McAuliffe taught at Concord High School in Concord, New Hampshire, and she was selected from about eleven thousand applicants to be the first teacher in space.

Stephanie Evans and her fifth-grade classmates at R. Dean Kilby Elementary School in Woodbridge, Virginia, were eager to watch the *Challenger* take off. They had made ice cream to celebrate the event. When a bright explosion filled the TV screen seventy-three seconds after liftoff, "our first response was 'That was neat!'" Stephanie recalls. "Then the teacher explained that all the astronauts were dead. There was a moment of quiet time. Nobody wanted ice cream."

EQUALITY IN THE CLASSROOM

In the 1970s and 1980s, the barriers that had kept certain American students out of school finally began to fall. Through new laws and programs, the Supreme Court, Congress, the Department of Education (created in 1979), and other government agencies worked to ensure that every child had equal opportunities for good schooling.

One new law guaranteed children with disabilities the right to "a publicly supported education suited to their needs." Public schools were required to design individual programs for these students and to teach them "in the least restrictive environment" possible. This meant that many students who had been formerly assigned to special education classes now joined other students in regular classrooms. Public schools were also required to provide access to students in wheelchairs.

With federal support, school districts also channeled funds and resources to programs for migrant children, children living in homeless shelters, and those living on the streets. Even foreign children whose parents were living illegally in the United States gained the right to free public education.

Many public schools began bilingual education programs, designed to provided instruction in their native languages to students with "limited English proficiency." For instance, children whose families spoke mainly Spanish at home could learn in both Spanish and English at school. The native language for many American students is, in fact, Spanish. But some large urban school districts, such as San Francisco, also teach immigrant children from more than one hundred countries.

A big boost for girls in school came with Title IX of the Education Amendments Act of 1972. This law said that public school students could not be excluded from programs or activities on account of their sex. Title IX had its biggest impact in the area of school sports. With the new law, equal funds were made available for boys' and girls' sports teams, as was scholarship money for male and female athletes. Before Title IX, fewer than three hundred thousand high school girls played competitive sports. By the end of the twentieth century, the number would rise to more than two million.

NEW FACES

The United States continued to welcome new immigrant groups. One group that arrived during the 1970s and 1980s was the Hmong. Originally from Laos and nearby areas in Southeast Asia, the Hmong had aided Americans during the war in Vietnam. Many were forced to flee their homes when U.S. forces withdrew from the region.

Maijue Xiong was born in a small village in Laos in 1972. In 1978 she flew to Los Angeles and entered kindergarten at Isla Vista Elementary School. She remembers:

> The first day was scary because I could not speak any English. Fortunately, my cousin, who had been in the United States for three years and spoke English, was in the same class with me. She led me to the playground where the children were playing. I was shocked to see so many faces of different colors. The Caucasian children shocked me the most. I had never seen people with blond hair before. . . . In class, I was introduced to coloring. I did not know how to hold a crayon or what it was for. My teacher had to show me how to color. I also learned the alphabet. This was the beginning of my lifelong goal to get an education.

Ia Vang Xiong and her family settled in Minnesota. She would later become one of the first Hmong to become a teacher in California. She says:

> I came to the United States when I was about twelve years old, so they had to put me in school right away. . . . I felt isolated, and I think I made myself feel like an outcast because I was afraid nobody would understand who I am. . . . I was always very quiet. But I tried studying very hard.

Ia Vang Xiong took English as a Second Language (ESL) classes with other Hmong students, but she joined the general group for one social studies class. She remembers:

> I was the only Hmong. I didn't understand one thing they said in that class. I sat in the back, and the teacher didn't know what to do with me either. . . . Now I [teach] students like that.

THE WORLD AT YOUR FINGERTIPS

Desktop-sized personal computers (PCs) became popular classroom tools in the 1980s. By the end of the twentieth century, students were using them for everything from basic arithmetic to complex scientific experiments.

Computers also helped students with disabilities to both learn and communicate. Some computers read printed material out loud to visually impaired students, for example, while students who were unable to use their hands could write messages on computer screens using verbal input devices.

First developed in the 1970s, the World Wide Web (also known as the Internet) entered many classrooms in the 1990s. The Web made it easy for students to gather information from many different sources, including other students. Schools like Axtell Park Middle School in Sioux Falls, South Dakota, put student projects on their own websites, with links to informational sites such as the Library of Congress and Public Television's Bill Nye, the Science Guy. The seventh graders at Moanalua Intermediate School in Honolulu, Hawaii, were responsible for maintaining their school's website.

A project called EarthKam, operated by the National Aeronautics and Space Administration (NASA), even brought space exploration into the classroom in the 1990s. Students involved in the project selected areas on earth to be photographed from space. Their choices were sent to space shuttle astronauts via satellite. The astronauts took the photographs using digital video cameras, then sent the pictures to NASA, which displayed them on its website.

THE POWER OF ONE

Technology could not replace one critical source of learning in the classroom—teachers. The 1988 movie *Stand and Deliver* paid tribute to one real-life teacher, Jaime Escalante. He taught Latino students in a poor Los Angeles school to master calculus and helped them pass an advanced placement exam to earn college credit.

Robert Pelka's story didn't make it to the movies, but he also made a difference in the lives of young people. In 1989 sixth-grade-teacher Pelka taught Latoya Hunter, a Jamaican immigrant living in the Bronx in New York City. In *The Diary of Latoya Hunter: My First Year in Junior High,* she writes:

> He didn't only teach me academic things. . . . He taught me how to be open-minded to all kinds of people. . . . The things he changed about me are innumerable. The world should know this man. He probably won't go down in any major history books but if this diary counts as a book of history, he just did.

Roberta Guaspari-Tzavaras was another inspiring teacher. Her success with violin students in the East Harlem section of New York

By the 1980s, children were using computers in the classroom.

City was portrayed in the movies *Small Wonders* (1996) and *Music of the Heart* (1999).

BILLION-STUDENT CLASSROOMS

On a warm October day in the mid-1990s, students at Cobb Middle School in Tallahassee, Florida, reported a maximum atmospheric temperature of eighty-four degrees Fahrenheit. On the same day, students at Integrovana Stredni Skola in the Czech Republic reported a maximum temperature of fifty-five degrees. Both schools were part of Global Learning and Observations to Benefit the Earth (GLOBE), a program created to help scientists assess changes in the world's climate.

The schools reported their findings via the Internet to the National Oceanic and Atmospheric Administration in Boulder, Colorado. The findings were combined with other data, turned into computerized images by NASA, and relayed to other GLOBE schools by television, computers, and other telecommunications systems. GLOBE schools also communicated with each other over the Internet.

The GLOBE students at Cobb Middle School and Integrovana Stredni Skola shared a classroom—not a real one with desks and blackboards but a virtual one, in which information was exchanged and students learned together. Imagine if progressive educators from the early 1900s and open classroom advocates from the 1970s somehow met. Suppose they decided to use twenty-first-century technology to bring the United States's fifty-three million schoolchildren and three million elementary and secondary school teachers into one giant, virtual classroom. What if they included students and teachers from around the world?

In the year 2000, only a few hundred one-room public schoolhouses were operating in the United States. One of them was the tiny school in Bloomfield, Montana, a classroom for only thirteen students. Their school looked much like a frontier schoolhouse of 1900. But with the help of new technology, the thirteen students had a billion virtual classmates. What will their school be like in 2050 or 3000?

Live and learn.

EARLY SCHOOL RULES AND LESSONS

YOUNG MAN'S COMPANION, **1717**
Wash your Hands always before you come to School.

THE AMERICAN TUTOR'S GUIDE, **1808**
A man overtaking a maid driving a flock of geese, said to her, how do you do, sweetheart? Where are you going with these 100 geese? No Sir, said she, I have not 100; but if I had [twice] as many, half as many, and seven geese and a half, I should have 100: How many had she? *Ans. 37*

LANCASTRIAN SCHOOL BOOK MANUAL, **1850**
The Book-Monitor, with the right hand hands the book to the pupil, who receives it with the right hand, with the back of the book to the left, and then passes it into the left hand, where it is held with the back upwards, and with the thumb extended at an angle of forty-five degrees with the edge of the book . . . , until a further order is given.

McGUFFEY'S ECLECTIC THIRD GRADE READER, **1853**
If you forget God when you are young, God may forget you when you are old.

THE COMMON-SCHOOL ARITHMETIC, **1857**
George Washington was born A.D. 1732. He was elected president when 57 years old, and died 10 years afterwards. In what year did he die?

HALFWAY SCHOOLHOUSE RULES FOR TEACHERS, MICHIGAN, **1872**
- Teachers each day will fill lamps, clean chimneys.
- Each teacher will bring a bucket of water and a scuttle of coal for the day's session.
- Men teachers may take one evening each week for courting purposes, or two evenings a week if they go to church regularly.
- Women teachers who marry or engage in unseemly conduct will be dismissed.
- The teacher who performs his labor faithfully and without fault for five years will be given an increase of twenty-five cents per week in his pay, providing the Board of Education approves.

BUREAU OF INDIAN AFFAIRS RULES FOR OPERATING INDIAN BOARDING SCHOOLS, **1890**
Pupils must be compelled to converse with each other in English, and should be properly rebuked or punished for persistent violation of this rule.

POLITE MANNERS FOR LITTLE MEN AND WOMEN, **1911**
Don't whistle in school.

SCHOOLHOUSES TO VISIT

FRIENDSHIP SCHOOL, CAMPBELLSVILLE, KENTUCKY
Originally located on the Cowherd Farm, this school was built about 1918. It is now a museum and classroom, located right behind the Taylor County High School.

GIBBS FARM MUSEUM SCHOOLHOUSE, ST. PAUL, MINNESOTA
Built in the 1870s, the schoolhouse is part of a restored farm. Visitors can spend a summer day learning the way students did in the nineteenth century.

HALFWAY SCHOOLHOUSE, EASTPOINTE, MICHIGAN
Built in 1872, this Victorian schoolhouse looks a lot like a church from the outside. Boys and girls entered from separate doorways and sat on opposite sides of the room.

LANESFIELD SCHOOL, JOHNSON COUNTY, KANSAS
Schoolchildren could see travelers on the Santa Fe Trail from the Lanesfield School, built in 1869. The school's interior was rebuilt in 1904, after being destroyed by lightning. Visitors can take part in penmanship lessons, spell-downs, and other activities in the school.

SANTA ANA SCHOOLHOUSE, SAN JOSÉ, CALIFORNIA
Built in 1872, the Santa Ana School was used by children in the local farming and ranching community of Hollister for about one hundred years. It has been moved to the San José Historical Museum, and the schoolhouse is visited by more than twenty-five thousand students a year.

SENECA SCHOOLHOUSE MUSEUM, POOLESVILLE, MARYLAND
A one-room, stone building, Seneca School was built in 1865. Visitors to the school can attend a nineteenth-century school day there, clustering around the potbellied stove and reciting lessons from McGuffey Readers.

STRAWBERRY SCHOOLHOUSE, STRAWBERRY, ARIZONA
This pine log schoolhouse was built in 1884 by cowboys and settlers in Arizona Territory. Well furnished with an organ and wallpaper, the schoolhouse was also the community's social center and church.

VOORLEZER'S HOUSE, RICHMOND TOWN, STATEN ISLAND, NEW YORK
This wooden structure, dating back to 1695, was the home of the Dutch community's *voorlezer* (lay minister and teacher). With a classroom on the first floor, the house is considered the oldest elementary school building in the United States.

SELECTED BIBLIOGRAPHY

Beals, Melba Pattillo. *Warriors Don't Cry.* New York: Pocket Books, 1994.

Bridges, Ruby. *Through My Eyes.* New York: Scholastic Press, 1999.

Calof, Rachel. *Rachel Calof's Story: Jewish Homesteader on the Northern Plains.* Bloomington, IN: Indiana University Press, 1995.

Chan, Sucheng. *Hmong Means Free: Life in Laos and America.* Philadelphia: Temple University Press, 1994.

Cleary, Beverly. *A Girl from Yamhill.* New York: William Morrow and Company, Inc., 1988.

Cohen, Sol, ed. *Education in the United States: A Documentary History.* Westport, CT: Greenwood Press, Inc., 1977.

Cremin, Lawrence A. *American Education: The Colonial Experience, 1607–1783.* New York: Harper & Row, 1970.

———. *American Education: The National Experience, 1783–1876.* New York: Harper & Row, 1980.

———. *The Transformation of the School: Progressivism in American Education, 1876–1957.* New York: Alfred A. Knopf, 1961.

Eggleston, Edward. *The Hoosier School-Master.* New York: Orange Judd and Company, 1871.

Hassebrock, Kenneth. *Rural Reminiscences: The Agony of Survival.* Ames, IA: Iowa State University Press, 1990.

Holden, Anna. *The Bus Stops Here: A Study of School Desegregation in Three Cities.* New York: Agathan Press, 1974.

Jacobs, Jane, ed. *A Schoolteacher in Old Alaska: The Story of Hannah Breece.* New York: Randon House, 1995.

Johnson, Clifton. *Old-Time Schools and School-Books*. New York: The Macmillan Co., 1925.

Katz, Jane, ed. *Messengers of the Wind: Native American Women Tell Their Life Stories*. New York: Ballantine Books, 1995.

Kaufman, Polly Welts. *Women Teachers on the Frontier*. New Haven, CT: Yale University Press, 1984.

Kismaric, Carole, and Marvin Heiferman. *Growing Up with Dick and Jane*. San Francisco: Collins Publishers, 1996.

Lockwood, George B. *The New Harmony Movement*. New York: Dover Publications, Inc., 1971.

Morris, Willie. *Good Old Boy: A Delta Boyhood*. Oxford, MS: Yoknapatawpha Press, Inc., 1980.

Sloane, Eric. *The Little Red Schoolhouse*. Garden City: Doubleday & Co., Inc., 1972.

Stanley, Jerry. *Children of the Dust Bowl: The True Story of the School at Weedpatch Camp*. New York: Crown Publishers, Inc., 1992.

Tyack, David B., Thomas James, and Aaron Benavot. *Law and the Shaping of Public Education, 1785–1954*. Madison, WI: University of Wisconsin Press, 1987.

Uchida, Yoshiko. *The Invisible Thread*. New York: Beech Tree Paperback, 1995.

Washington, Booker T. *Up from Slavery*. 1901. Reprint, New York: Dodd, Mead & Company, 1965.

Wilder, Laura Ingalls. *Little Town on the Prairie*. New York: Harper & Row, 1941.

INDEX

ACKNOWLEDGMENTS

Photographs and illustrations used with permission of: Fred Hulstrand History in Pictures Collection, NDIRS-NDSU, Fargo, N.D., p. 2; © Bettmann/Corbis, pp. 6, 13, 54, 60; Brown Brothers, pp. 8, 19, 48; Hulton Getty Picture Library/Archive Photos, pp. 16, 21; Leonard Everett Fisher, Illustrator, p. 18; North Wind Picture Archives, pp. 22, 23, 28, 42, 43; © Corbis, pp. 26, 35; DeWitt Historical Society/Archive Photos, p. 30; Library of Congress, pp. 32, 41, 49, 52; Hawaii State Archives, p. 36; Dictionary of American Portraits, p. 38; Popperfoto/Archive Photos, p. 46; Minnesota Historical Society/Corbis, p. 51; National Archives (NDWNS-210-G-A451), p. 55; Schomburg Center for Research in Black Culture, p. 62; Archive Photos, pp. 64, 75; AP Photo/Corcoran Gallery, p. 67; © Ted Streshinsky/Corbis, p. 69; © Leif Skoogfors/Corbis, p. 70; © Owen Franken/Corbis, p. 72; Control Data, p. 80.
Front cover: © Bettmann/Corbis